Supporting Children with

Autistic Spectrum Disorder

Hull Learning Services

David Fulton Publishers

David Fulton Publishers Ltd
The Chiswick Centre, 414 Chiswick High Road, London W4 5TF

www.fultonpublishers.co.uk
www.onestopeducation.co.uk

First published in Great Britain by Hull Learning Services 2004
Reprinted 2005
10 9 8 7 6 5 4 3 2

David Fulton Publishers is a division of Granada Learning Limited, part of ITV plc

Copyright © David Fulton Publishers Ltd 2004

British Library Cataloguing in Publication Data
A catalogue record for this book is available from the British Library.

ISBN 1 84312 219 7

Typeset by Matrix Creative, Wokingham
Printed and bound in Great Britain

Contents

Foreword

This book was produced in partnership with services based in Hull, the Special Educational Needs Support Service, the Hull City Psychological Service, the Northcott ASD Outreach Service and the Hull and East Riding Community Health NHS Trust and written by:

Colleen O'Connell: Northcott ASD Outreach Teacher
Ruth Dance: Educational Psychologist
Ven Delasaux: Children's Centre Nursery Classroom
Elizabeth Morling: Early years transition co-ordinator
Susan Miller: Senior Educational Psychologist
Kathryn Ranby: Speech and Language Therapist
Pauline Russell: Portage supervisor
Carole Stitt: Educational Psychologist
Karen Stockman: Speech and Language Therapist

Edited by Colleen O'Connell, Elizabeth Morling and Carole Stitt

With thanks to senior adviser John Hill for his support and encouragement throughout the development of this series.

It is one of a series of eleven titles providing an up-to-date overview of special educational needs for SENCOs, teachers and other professionals and parents.

The books were produced in response to training and information needs, raised by teachers, support staff and parents in Hull. The aim of these books is to raise awareness and address many of the issues involved in creating inclusive environments.

Owing to the nature of the difficulties presented by the condition of an ASD, it is inevitable that there are overlaps between the discrete areas of the book. The authors feel that it would be of benefit to the reader for certain points to be re-emphasised as the book is to be dipped into as necessary.

For details of other titles and how to order, please see page 49.

Introduction

Recent government policy, as described in the Green Paper 'Excellence for All Children' (DfEE 1997), has indicated that local education authorities should be working towards meeting the needs of the majority of pupils with special educational needs in mainstream schools. Given that there is a trend to identify more pupils with an ASD and for local education authorities to seek to maximise inclusion, it is reasonable to assume that the proportion will increase.

Implications of the Disability Discrimination Act (1995) as amended by the SEN and Disability Act 2001 (SENDA 2001)

Part one of the Act:

- strengthens the right of children to be educated in mainstream schools;
- requires LEAs to arrange for parents and/or children with SEN to be provided with advice on SEN matters, and also a means of settling disputes with schools and LEAs (parent partnership services and mediation/conciliation schemes);
- requires schools to tell parents where they are making special educational provision for their child and allows schools to request a statutory assessment of a pupil's needs.

In accordance with the above Act LEAs and schools must:

- not treat disabled pupils less favourably;
- make reasonable adjustments so that the physical, sensory and learning needs of disabled pupils are accommodated, in order that they are not put at a substantial disadvantage to pupils who are not disabled;
- plan strategically and make progress in increasing not only physical accessibility to the schools' premises and to the curriculum, but also to improve the delivery of written information in an accessible way to disabled pupils (i.e. access to the curriculum via oral means, as well as the written word).

Definition of disability

- The Disability Discrimination Act uses a very broad definition of 'disability'. A person has a disability if he or she has a physical or mental impairment that has a substantial and long-term adverse effect on his or her ability to carry out normal day-to-day activities.

- The DDA definition of disability covers physical disabilities and sensory impairments, such as those affecting sight or hearing and learning difficulties.

The inclusive school

A school that is educationally inclusive is an effective school. An educationally inclusive school has the following features:

- an ethos of inclusion that is understood by staff, parents, governors, pupils and the local community;

- achievements of all pupils are valued, recognised and celebrated;

- improving teaching and learning for all pupils is a constant concern to senior managers;

- the well-being of all pupils matters; their attitudes, values and behaviour are constantly challenged and developed;

- staff, pupils and parents treat each other with respect;

- senior managers put into place actions and strategies to ensure that all pupils make better progress.

Schools should offer an inclusive curriculum, in the broadest sense, that is appropriate for different groups of pupils. Each school should have appropriate systems in place to identify the needs of different groups of pupils and ensure that its provision meets these needs.

Essentially therefore, the five principles developing a more inclusive curriculum require a commitment to:

- valuing all learners;

- setting suitable learning challenges for groups and individuals;

- responding to pupils' diverse learning needs;

- overcoming potential barriers to learning and assessment for individuals and groups of pupils;

- making the best use of resources.

Inclusion for pupils with an ASD

Pupils with an Autistic Spectrum Disorder (ASD) are mainly educated in mainstream schools with a minority being placed in special schools. The condition is such that these pupils can usually access the curriculum: guidelines from the Code of Practice (2001) recognise that

> Most children with special educational needs have strengths and difficulties in one, some or all of the areas of speech, language and communication. Their communication needs may be both diverse and complex. The range will encompass… those who demonstrate features within the autistic spectrum….

These children may require some, or all, of the following:

- help in acquiring, comprehending and using language;
- help to use different means of communication confidently and competently for a range of purposes including formal situations;
- flexible teaching arrangements;
- help with processing language, memory and reasoning skills;
- help in organising and co-ordinating oral and written language.

Children who demonstrate features of moderate, severe or profound learning difficulties may require specific programmes to aid progress in cognition and learning. Such requirements may also apply to… those on the autistic spectrum.

These children may require some, or all, of the following:

- help and support in acquiring literacy skills;
- help in organising and co-ordinating spoken and written English to aid cognition;
- help with sequencing and organisational skills;
- help with problem solving and developing concepts;
- programmes to aid improvement of fine and gross motor competencies.

Definition

An Autistic Spectrum Disorder is biologically based, and is characterised by a 'triad of impairments' (Wing 1996). This affects a person's ability to use and understand social communication and social interaction, and to be flexible in their thinking, behaviour and use of imagination. In addition, there are frequently implications in connection with motivation, generalisation and hypo- or hyper-sensitivity to sensory stimuli.
It is widely recognised that pupils across the full ability range may have this lifelong disorder and many may have additional special educational needs.

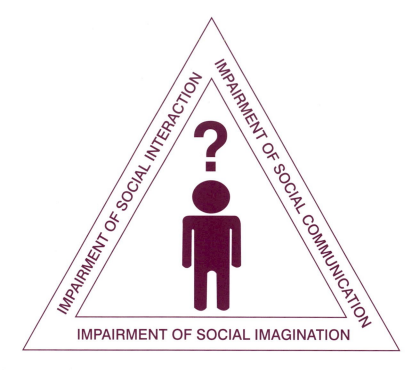

Throughout this book the term Autistic Spectrum Disorder (ASD) will be used to refer to all pupils who are at some point along the autistic continuum and therefore, will include those with Asperger's Syndrome, Autism, semantic pragmatic disorder, and pathological demand avoidance syndrome. These difficulties are seen as a continuum and the degree to which pupils are affected will vary significantly.

Pupils with Asperger's Syndrome are still characterised by the triad of impairments but tend to have average or above average intelligence and will have fewer problems with language. They may speak fluently but their words can still sound formal or stilted.

The following three chapters identify the key impairments that are associated with autism, these include difficulties with social communication, interaction and imagination. Each will be followed by a series of suggestions/activities to support each of the impairments.

Impairment of social communication

Communication allows us to make our wants and needs known and to share our feelings, thoughts and ideas with others. It is what helps us to learn from relationships and make connections with the world around us and the people in it. Every pupil or young person with an autistic spectrum disorder will have some degree of difficulty with communication.

The skills involved in communication

In order to communicate effectively we need to develop skills in a number of areas.

Processing and using verbal communication involves:

- the ability to listen and attend to relevant information;
- the ability to understand words, phrases and sentences;
- the ability to understand the literal and non-literal meanings behind spoken words and ideas;
- the ability to express our ideas with spoken words and to speak each word clearly;
- the ability to construct sentences and use English grammar correctly;
- the ability to use language for a range of purposes such as requesting, commenting, questioning, discussing, and having conversations;
- the ability to use language appropriately in a social setting, i.e. what to say, when to say it and to whom;
- the skills involved in verbal interaction with others such as continuing the topic, monitoring topic shift and conversational repair (adjusting the content of the conversation if the speaker is aware that the listener is not responding appropriately).

Interpreting and using non-verbal communication involves a number of skills:

- engaging in 'joint attention', such as looking and listening together or sharing in the same moment or event with someone, with mutual enjoyment and meaning;
- using looking and eye contact both as a speaker and a listener;
- understanding and using facial expression;
- understanding and using spontaneous gestures and body posture to communicate or emphasise meaning;
- being able to interpret and use 'prosodic' features, i.e. how intonation, volume and rate of speech helps to convey meaning and emotion;
- having the ability to take turns in social activities and conversations;
- the ability to initiate conversation and attract someone's attention;

- the ability to change the topic or style of a conversation to suit the needs or interests of the listener;
- the ability to understand implied meanings and read between the lines of what the other person is saying.

Language and communication difficulties associated with an ASD

Pupils with an ASD will have difficulties in a number of areas:

Understanding language

- There may be failure to respond, or the pupil does not seem interested when spoken to. The pupil can be totally unaware that he/she is expected to listen unless specifically prompted to do so, e.g. in a group or whole class discussion.
- Unusual responses to auditory stimulation can result in sensory defensiveness. The pupil may attempt to block out confusing sounds or noises by covering his/her ears or by showing signs of distress.
- The vocabulary and grammar of spoken language becomes difficult to understand as it increases in length and complexity.
- Many pupils with an ASD are 'visual learners', i.e. they find it easier to understand visually presented information than verbally presented information.
- Information tends to be processed slowly. There is often a time delay between hearing what someone says and being able to formulate a response.
- Understanding of language is over-literal and concrete. Implied or ambiguous meanings can be confusing, e.g. sarcasm, idioms and synonyms.
- Confusion arises when people talk too loudly, too fast or use too many words.

Communication

- There is an absence or a reduction in the desire to communicate with others.
- The pupil may fail to compensate for the lack of spoken language, e.g. use of natural gesture, with the exception of pulling someone, or using his/her hand as a tool.
- The development of speech may be absent or delayed.
- The pupil may only communicate socially at a basic level, i.e. to satisfy a need or gain information.
- The pupil may develop some spoken language, but fail to use this for the purposes of communication with others.
- The pupil may be quick to echo speech or repeat 'chunks' of language spoken by other people, often without understanding the meaning.
- The content of speech tends to be one-sided and can be repetitive.

- The pupil may experience difficulties with appropriate conversational turn-taking.
- The pupil may accept or make approaches to others, but lack the skills to follow these through.

Strategies to help the pupil with an ASD to communicate more effectively

Helping pupils to initiate and respond to communication

- Being 'face-to-face' will encourage eye-contact and promote positive interaction.
- Observe what catches the pupil's interest and follow his/her lead and use this interest to encourage joint attention, motivate and develop learning.
- Teach turn-taking skills. Play-turn taking games and encourage more verbal pupils to take turns to speak and listen during conversation.
- Set up structured social communication skills groups to encourage pupils to take turns, listen and communicate with others.
- Help pupils to notice and interpret non-verbal communication such as facial expression and body language.

Helping pupils to understand what is said

- Say the pupil's name before communicating to help establish joint attention.
- Use physical prompts to gain attention and to guide the pupil through new experiences. Physical prompts should be phased out as soon as the task can be carried out independently.
- Reduce language, keep it simple, concrete and well within the pupil's level of understanding. Use key words and short sentences. Clarify ambiguous language for older pupils.
- Use a slower rate of speech to allow the pupil time to process the information.
- Be prepared to wait longer for the pupil to respond to questions or instructions – at least 15 seconds.
- Label objects, people and events. Use specific names and avoid words like 'this', 'it', 'he', 'she' 'there'. Match labels or symbols to concrete objects or to activities while they are in progress.
- Ask fewer direct questions and increase comments, e.g. 'I see a car' rather than 'What is it?'
- Use visual forms of communication to support verbal language. These need to be appropriate for the pupil's level of development and can include real objects, pictures, symbols and visual or written timetables.
- Break down longer instructions using two or three simple sentences instead of one complicated one.

- Put information in a logical sequence within sentences and give instructions in the order they will happen.
- Direct the pupil's attention at an individual level rather than relying on whole class instructions.
- Interpret the pupil's actions and behaviours so they can hear the language they are unable to express themselves.
- Tell the pupil what to do rather than what not to do.
- Be aware that the pupil will have difficulty picking up on non-verbal communication.
- Help the pupil to identify meanings; are they:
  - non-literal (idioms, sarcasm, jokes…);
  - true or false;
  - real or pretend;
  - fact or opinion?

Helping pupils to communicate with others

- Be prepared to wait in order to give the pupil a chance to initiate communication.
- Interpret any attempts to communicate and be aware that the pupil is often communicating through their non-verbal reactions and behaviours as well as their verbal behaviours.
- Give the pupil reasons to communicate by not anticipating their every need.
- Develop communication through picture and symbol exchange – PECS.
- Give verbal choices to help the pupil respond to questions, e.g. 'Crisps or biscuit?' rather than 'What do you want to eat?'
- Encourage the pupil to make requests using highly motivating objects and activities as an incentive to communicate with others.
- Model language as if you were the pupil talking, e.g. 'I want a drink' rather than 'Do you want a drink?'
- For pupils who are unable to answer questions, change them into statements, e.g. 'James made a…' instead of 'What did you make?' or 'The boy is crying because…' instead of 'Why is the boy crying?'
- Encourage the pupil to communicate in new situations and for different reasons.
- Be aware that the pupil may need to be taught how to ask for help and clarification.
- Encourage appropriate conversational skills; how to:
  - begin and end the conversation appropriately;
  - stay on topic;
  - introduce a new topic;
  - take a turn and hand over the turn;
  - repair conversation breakdown.

Impairment of social interaction

There is a wide variation in the level of social interaction observed, depending on cognitive ability, level of language skills, personality and situation. Difficulties arise owing to impaired understanding of the two-way nature of communication and interaction and how other people think and feel.

Pupils with an ASD may:

- seem to prefer their own company, showing signs of stress if others come too near;
- want the friendship of others but be socially awkward;
- find it difficult to look at the other person;
- not pick up the non-verbal social cues of mood, availability, social status;
- be over-familiar with teachers and strangers or over-formal with peers;
- not read the non-verbal signals involved in turn-taking in conversations;
- talk like a 'little professor' in great detail about their own, often obscure, interests;
- speak in a rather monotonous tone of voice, without varying inflection, speed or volume;
- be able to make friends initially, but fail to have the skills to maintain them;
- be vulnerable to bullying.

Strategies can be developed to support the pupil in a number of ways

- If contact with others seems stressful, a very gradual approach may be necessary in order to desensitise the pupil. Tolerating the physical proximity of another pupil may have to be built up in small steps.
- Using a small steps approach, gradually increase the pupil's tolerance of playing and working in proximity to others.
- Provide a workstation where the pupil may work for at least some of the time to reduce stress and minimise distractions.
- Practise new social situations with a sympathetic adult beforehand.
- Teach explicitly rules and conventions of conversation, e.g. how to begin and end, how to tell if another person is interested, how to take turns.
- Teach how to recognise a person's social status; unfamiliar adults and teachers expect to be spoken to in a different way from peers or family.

- Set definite limits on when, where and for how long the pupil may talk about a specific obsessional topic. Initially, use visual prompts such as gesture or symbol to remind the pupil, fading to more unobtrusive methods such as a code-word or phrase.

- Model normal conversations and use role-play, giving feedback to raise awareness. Use video-tapes of real-life situations or soap-operas to provide training and make the rules explicit. Use a structured social skills programme such as 'The Social Use of Language' (Rinaldi, NFER) to break down the skills of conversation into manageable targets.

- Provide more structure at break-times, e.g. a support assistant may involve pupils in playground games with simple rules or in a lunchtime computer club.

- Find another pupil/adult to escort the pupil with an ASD between classes. Have a simple plan/map of how to get to the next classroom.

- Have a clear anti-bullying policy, which is regularly monitored. Provide simple, clear guidelines on how to avoid situations and what to do if things go wrong.

- It may help to have a regular, set opportunity to get support from a particular member of staff, e.g. a mentor.

- Teach the pupil with an ASD particular behaviours to deal with specific situations, e.g. how to behave if someone is cross with you. The use of social stories may be useful in this context.

- Within the classroom routine, develop a series of 'jobs' which the pupil may do with, or for, other members of the class. Such tasks may be taking the register, taking messages, giving out drinks, handing out the books etc. Successful completion of these activities will also raise the pupil's self-esteem.

- All adults who may meet the pupil require some basic information on Autistic Spectrum Disorder and the specific needs of the pupil.

- Keep at a distance which is comfortable to the pupil.

- Use a quiet tone of voice to the pupil.

- Continue with the interaction whether or not the pupil is giving eye contact.

- Use a form of communication that the pupil understands.

- Assess whether the pupil is likely to be able to understand and respond to a request.

Friends Group

This programme has been designed by a Speech and Language Therapist to support a group of 3–4 pupils. The group meets regularly with the support of two adults who model appropriate behaviour. The pupils are taught the non-verbal skills for becoming 'good listeners' and are encouraged to become 'good friends' through developing skills such as, using social greetings, remembering important things about other people, sharing ideas, etc.

Circle of Friends

This is a useful strategy, developed in the USA, for the development of social skills in pupils with special educational needs. The 'Circle' should meet regularly, with the intention of developing and implementing strategies to support the individual pupil at break and lunchtimes. If such a group is to be established, careful planning and management is necessary.

Social Stories

These stories were the idea of Carol Gray from the USA. Individual stories are written for pupils, which will teach them the appropriate way to behave or react in a particular social situation. So, for example, a story about how to line up for lunch could be written for a pupil who always wants to push to the front of the queue. Social Stories are also useful tools for the preparation for transitions, such as moving classes or schools. They are excellent for those pupils who understand simple sentences, and can also be written using symbols or photographs. There are published examples of social stories, but they should always be written on an individual basis, following the set formula.

Nurture groups

These may be used as an extra resource for pupils to have the opportunity to develop social interaction skills within a small supportive group, but be mindful of inclusion issues.

Impairment of social imagination

Impairments of flexible thinking, coherence and executive function associated with autism mean that pupils with an ASD may display a number of characteristics.

- They may have difficulty playing imaginatively with toys and equipment. Play may be restricted to specific interests such as lining up the dolls or cars.

- They may have difficulty developing 'make believe' games. Therefore the pretend game of 'Batman and Robin' could, in fact, simply be re-enacting an episode they have seen previously, which they are unable to develop further using their own ideas.

- They may become reliant on routines and have a need to keep things safe and familiar. Pupils may become anxious or distressed if there are any changes, no matter how slight they may appear, e.g. changes in classroom displays, daily routines.

- They may have difficulty creating something entirely from their imagination.

- They may have difficulty understanding another person's perspective.

- They may have difficulty making sense of everyday experiences, especially in understanding their social and cultural meaning.

- They may have difficulty generalising learning to new situations.

- They may take things literally and perceive things in definite black and white terms, with no grey area in between. The pupil who is told it is 'raining cats and dogs' for example, will expect to see exactly that, or if directed to 'go to the office', may do so easily but not know to come back again.

- They may have difficulty understanding abstract concepts. Those things that can be seen or touched will be understood, but for concepts such as 'furniture' or 'heavier', for example, it is difficult for pupils with an ASD to attach a visual representation in their head.

- They may have difficulty problem solving outside of cued rote responses.

- They may have difficulty widening their interests from their narrow obsessions.

- They may have difficulty remembering personal memories and events outside the context in which they occurred and making connections with existing knowledge. However, they often have an extensive memory for factual information learned by rote.

- They may have difficulty focusing attention outside their own areas of interest.

- They may have difficulty understanding 'cause and effect'.

There are a number of strategies, that will support the pupil

- Use visual cues such as pictures and diagrams to support learning.

- Use a visual timetable to prepare the pupil for any changes in routine.

- Develop social stories to prepare the pupil for imminent changes such as a change of class or teacher.

- Use photographs to prepare the pupil for a new school, new classmates.

- Use similar formats and routines to increase familiarity and predictability.

- Simplify language and allow processing time.

- Provide frameworks such as storyboards and 'cloze' exercises to aid organisation and planning of independent writing.

- Teach the use of cues such as key words or pictures to aid recall.

- Allow time for the 'over-learning' and practice of new skills.

- Ensure that opportunities to teach the generalisation of skills are provided.

- Teach 'play' skills by modelling.

- Use the pupil's 'special interest' as a reward or motivator for working and good behaviour.

- Teach older pupils who have verbal skills the meaning behind common ambiguous sayings.

- Use flow diagrams to teach consequences of actions/cause and effect.

Sensory difficulties

It is evident from reading the personal accounts of people with an ASD that most experience difficulties in processing sensory information.

They may:

- be hyper-sensitive to sensory stimuli for example:
  - become distressed by the particular volume or pitch of sounds.
  - be distracted by visual information/patterns/movements: eye contact may actually be 'painful';
  - find touch, certain textures and changes in temperature uncomfortable/ painful;
  - find some smells and perfumes overpowering, no matter how mild they appear to others;
  - dislike the taste of anything other than very bland foods.

- be hypo-sensitive to sensory stimuli for example:
  - look intensely at lights/patterns/objects;
  - like to listen to certain sounds and vibrations close to their ear;
  - not obviously react to pain and injuries;
  - like certain strong smells;
  - enjoy strong tastes (both edible and non-edible!).

- fluctuate from day to day, or even hour to hour, between hypo- and hyper-sensitivity to certain stimuli;
  - demonstrate behaviour which is related to sensory perceptual difficulties.
  - be able to only process information from one sensory channel at a time ('mono-channelled');
  - have a fragmented/distorted perception of objects, people and situations;
  - be easily distracted;
  - become increasingly withdrawn as they go into 'shutdown' due to sensory overload.

There are a number of strategies which can be used to help the pupil

- Use observations to find out what sensory stimulation the pupil finds difficult/likes/dislikes and talk to the family/carers about this.
- Where possible, remove sensory stimulation which is distressing/distracting, and re-introduce it carefully and gradually, using a small-steps approach.
- Be sensitive to the fluctuations in sensory processing difficulties.

Behaviour

Pupils with an ASD may behave inappropriately through lack of understanding rather than being deliberately 'naughty'. A number of considerations may be necessary in order to develop appropriate behaviour.

- Using ASD-specific behaviour management techniques has been proven to be beneficial to behaviour management in general.

- Behaviour and obsessions are often symptoms of anxiety, so look for the underlying cause before reacting to the pupil.

- In order to alleviate some of the anxiety shown by pupils with an ASD, it may be useful to utilise their strengths.

- Try to provide a consistent daily routine or focus on activities with predictable outcomes: stability is very important for pupils with an ASD.

- Give examples of how to cope in certain situations. Think about providing a special flag or object to hold when it's their turn to speak/take part.

- Try to structure free choice activities for a pupil with an ASD. This is often a confusing and frightening experience for them and they may need to be gradually introduced over a period of time.

- Always use a calm, clear voice: pupils with an ASD may become excited and over-stimulated by strong reactions or raised voices.

- Talk to others in the class about the difficulties experienced by pupils with an ASD. They may not fully understand the extent of their difficulties but it is important, so that they begin to understand the nature of the difficulty.

- Remember that although pupils with an ASD may appear to listen and understand what is said to them, they may not respond in the correct way. Target the pupil by using name or touch to focus his/her attention and by repeating group instructions to him/her on an individual basis.

- Try to vary the person who gives the instructions, so that the pupil learns to respond to a range of instructions/pupils/helpers.

- Pupils with an ASD may have difficulty anticipating the consequences of their actions. Make these clear by writing them down, or showing the consequences using symbols/flow diagrams.

- Use visual cues and clues – visual timetables are particularly effective in helping the pupil cope with what comes next.

- Keep language as simple as possible and be prepared to break down instructions into smaller components. Be specific when using instructions, e.g. 'Quiet please, sit down.'

- Use rewards for appropriate responses/behaviour and respond to attempts at communication.

- Try to teach the pupil that certain activities only take place in certain places (flapping, shouting, rocking) and give space for these or a special 'time out' for reward.

- Although structures and routines are vital to the well-being of a pupil with an ASD they can also become a problem in themselves. Build some flexibility into daily routines – it can be something simple like a different cup, chair or song. Keep testing the boundaries in a sensitive and controlled way until the pupil learns that changes aren't always confusing and frightening.

- If the pupil begins to establish obsessive routines, then try and intervene before things get out of hand, e.g. warn them that equipment/books will go away in two minutes.

- Provide distraction-free work access, e.g. desk facing a blank wall not situated near a window. Be aware of the environment and try to identify triggers that may provoke undesirable reactions.

- Work on developing independence by choosing tasks/activities that have in-built success.

- Use visual timetables to teach work first, then play.

- Model appropriate behaviours and prompt them through new tasks, e.g. by a hand-over-hand method.

Whole school implications

Schools should give consideration to pupils with an ASD in their SEN policy. Schools are complex systems; staff working within them need to consider how to plan together to provide a consistent environment which reflects the pupil's particular needs and is conducive to their well-being.

When a pupil with an ASD joins a mainstream school, it is helpful to make a number of considerations in order to meet the needs of pupils with the Triad of Impairments, i.e. social interaction, social communication and social imagination.

- The pupil with an ASD will encounter many people in school, who will need to have an understanding of their condition. These include:

  head teacher
  SENCO
  class teacher/form teacher
  support staff
  classmates
  subject teachers
  lunchtime supervisors
  clerical staff
  caretaker
  drivers and escorts
  visiting professionals
  school governors
  parent helpers.

In order to develop staff awareness:

- it is important that all members of the school staff be given information about the pupil and awareness training in autism;
- all staff should understand the reasons for agreed strategies and the importance of a consistent approach.

- One person should co-ordinate information about the pupil, usually the SENCO. In a large secondary school, it is also useful to have one liaison teacher from each subject area.

- It is important that a member of staff with whom the pupil has frequent contact is identified as having a particular responsibility for that pupil, e.g. the class teacher or form teacher.

- Staff require information about the individual needs of the particular pupil or pupils with an ASD who attend the school (useful information can be gained from the parents).

- Pupils, and possibly other parents, may need to know something about the pupil with an ASD and understand how best to help him or her. Pupils could cover this in PSHE.

- Priorities for the pupil with an ASD might be different from those for pupils of the same age.

- Staff should decide together in which areas of school life the pupil might need different considerations/planning from others.

- The planning of space is important to meet the following needs:
  - social skills training;
  - a quiet place to go;
  - a safe place to be at playtimes and lunchtimes, as these are frequently the most difficult times of the day;
  - clearly defined space for personal belongings.

- A system of review needs to be established prior to the start of the placement – initially, this may have to be daily.

- Individual targets need to be small and may need adjusting weekly.

- IEP reviews need to be held with the parents and pupils, to look at progress and set new targets.

Appendix 2 'What is an Autistic Spectrum Disorder?' provides a brief overview of an ASD which can be handed out to staff with encouragement to read the rest of the book at their convenience.

Transitions

Pupils with an ASD find it difficult moving from one situation to another. A number of considerations can be made in order to support the pupil.

- It is important to make it visually clear to the pupil what happens and where.
- Anticipate and plan for likely difficulties.
- 'Walk' the pupil through new routines.
- Develop appropriate strategies to enable the pupil to move from one area of school to another.
- Another pupil could be used to accompany the pupil with an ASD in transition.
- A map or visual photographs could be given of where to go next.
- The movement/noise can be frightening. Consideration should be given to the pupil leaving the lesson slightly earlier or later than the rest of the class.
- Secondary pupils should be reminded of where they are going towards the end of a lesson with the use of a visual timetable or diary.
- The rules for behaviour and class procedure should be consistent throughout the school.
- The pupil should be given advance notice of change and be prepared for this.
- Primary pupils should make visits to a new class towards the end of the academic year and spend some teaching time with the new teacher.
- Photographs could be given of the new classroom, with the pupil sitting in their new place.
- Information regarding successful strategies should be passed to the next teacher.
- Teach pupils to say when they need help or do not understand.
- Create a balance between tasks which the pupil finds difficult and those which can be done more easily.

Support staff: roles and responsibilities

Support staff should:

Have a clear understanding of their roles and responsibilities:

- have a knowledge of their job description;
- maintain a professional demeanour with parents;
- be aware of school policies with regard to behaviour, anti-bullying, Child Protection;
- respect the confidentiality of information for all pupils.

Be aware of channels of communication within the school:

- ensure that information provided by parents is given to the appropriate member of staff – class teacher, SENCO;
- ensure that recommendations, communications or reports from outside agencies are passed to the teacher and SENCO;
- ensure that information given to parents is with the knowledge of the class teacher;
- ensure that there is a mechanism for disseminating information to support staff about school activities, e.g. daily diary, staff room notice board.

Be recognised as valued members of a team:

- participate in the planning and monitoring process.

Be encouraged to make use of their personal skills:

- share skills, e.g. ICT, creative skills.

Be supported with appropriate on-going professional development:

- observe and learn from other professionals in school and in other establishments;
- undertake training in school and through external courses.

Encourage the pupil's independence at all times:

- by developing independent work skills;
- independent self-help skills;
- personal organisation.

Support staff: guidelines for working with pupils

Avoid	But instead…
Sitting next to the pupil at all times	work with other pupils, whilst keeping an eye on the pupil you are assigned to.
Offering too close an oversight during breaks and lunchtimes	encourage interaction with peers or allow the pupil to be solitary, follow his/her own interests and allow him/her to relax.
Collecting equipment for the pupil or putting it away	encourage the pupil to carry this out with independence, e.g. ensuring drawers are clearly labelled.
Completing a task for a pupil	ensure work is at an appropriate level and is carried out with minimal support (note any support given).
Using language inappropriate to the pupil	give short instructions at the pupil's level of development, with visual prompts.
Making unnecessary allowances for the pupil	establish what is required using appropriate strategies and have expectations that a task is to be completed.
Cluttered areas	provide a clear, predictable learning environment.
Tolerating undesirable behaviour	observe the pupil; determine reasons for behaviour and consider if changes can be made.
Making unrealistic demands on the pupil	ensure instructions are at the appropriate level and the goals are achievable.
Making decisions for the pupil	give the pupil opportunities to develop choice-making skills by providing structure and restricted choices.
The pupil becoming dependent on his/her support assistant	encourage independent behaviour and work.

Classroom management

The needs of pupils will vary greatly but the following may help to structure the classroom and reduce anxiety for the pupil.

Structure

- Pupils with an ASD need a structured environment that is predictable and offers routines.
- It is important to have visually clear boundaries for specific activities, e.g. this area is for work, this is for drink time.
- Structure the pupil's day by the use of a visual timetable, pictures or symbols, which shows what happens at each part of the day.
- Diaries can be used to outline the timetable for the day for pupils with reading skills.
- Indicate changes that are to take place in the timetable.
- Free choice can cause anxiety: give restricted choice or direct, using visual prompts.
- Develop routines for times that the pupil finds stressful.
- Activities must always have a clear start and finish.
- The pupil should always know and be explicitly (told in an appropriate way):
  - Where I have to be
  - What I have to do
  - How much I have to do
  - The time I will be finished
  - What I have to do next
- Provide the pupil with space for their belongings.
- Provide an area to work (possibly a workstation) which is as distraction free as possible, e.g. away from noise, windows, displays.
- Make available the equipment the pupil needs for the activity within this workspace whilst encouraging independent organisation where possible.
- Find a way of showing the pupil how much work has to be done, e.g. within the work area have a 'work to complete' tray and a 'work completed' tray.
- Use a timer to indicate how time is passing and that the work has to be completed within that time.
- Acknowledge anxieties and reduce pressure accordingly.
- Pupils are likely to need support to generalise new skills into different settings and in linking different bits of learning coherently into a whole.

Communication

- Consider alternative methods of ensuring that the pupil understands what is expected.
- Use photographs, symbols and drawings.
- Use photographs and videos to teach sequences of events.
- Do not tease even in a good-natured way – it will be taken literally and interpreted as criticism.
- Avoid negatives – tell the pupil what to do rather than what not to do.
- Do not overload the pupil with information.
- Use a slow rate of speech and give the pupil time to process the information.
- Avoid ambiguities.

Teaching

- Provide activities that build on the pupil's strengths.
- Provide opportunities for breaks within an activity, which is relaxing to the pupil, e.g. playing music.
- Give clear rules and be consistent.
- Reduce the amount of language given; be precise and concrete.
- Tell the pupil what to expect.
- Always forewarn of a change.
- Mean what you say and follow it through.
- Consider a small-steps approach to certain activities, starting at the pupil's level, e.g. if going to assembly is an issue, start with a few minutes at first and slowly build up the time.
- Teach the rules, e.g. how to line up, how to sit in the dining hall.
- Indicate boundaries by the use of a red line (portable or painted on the ground).
- Teach waiting and turn-taking skills.
- Ensure you've got the pupil's attention – begin with his/her name.
- Do not assume that the individual is attending to you particularly in a group situation; gain attention, for example, by touching the pupil's arm.
- Avoid confrontations with the pupil.
- Use the pupil's interests, 'obsessions' as rewards; include in the visual timetable.
- Give opportunities for exercise on a regular basis.
- Provide clearly defined breaks between structured activities.
- Consider the pupil's tolerance for other pupils in close proximity when considering seating positions – slowly develop the pupil's ability to sit more closely to others.

Accessing the curriculum

Pupils with an ASD will access the National Curriculum, which is differentiated through teaching strategies addressed throughout this book and more specifically below.

English

Speaking and listening

The impairment of social communication for pupils with an ASD will present great difficulties in this area. Detailed considerations are given in the relevant chapter (Impairment of social communication).

Reading

Pupils will have strengths and weaknesses in this area.

- Some pupils will have an interest in books and others will not.
- Language delays may hinder progress in reading but should not be a barrier to the introduction of the reading process.
- Pupils may learn letter sounds and names but further phonic skills such as blending may be difficult.
- In general the visual skills of a pupil with an ASD allow them to learn words through a whole word approach.
- The high level of visual skills may enable a pupil to immediately recognise words without needing to decode, but this can mask difficulties with comprehension.

There are a number of strategies which can be considered:
- Develop interest through flap books, pop-up books, noisy books.
- Help pupils make their own books about their interests, differentiated according to their age and ability.
- Use repetitive stories.
- Use concrete examples, e.g. puppets or toy animals, to give meaning to text.
- Encourage relating the picture to the text.
- A whole word approach may be more successful in preference to a phonic approach when learning new words.
- Use symbols to support reading, if appropriate.
- Pupils may relate more easily to non-fiction material.
- Use computer programs as an additional resource.
- Develop understanding and inference through comprehension exercises.

Handwriting

- Clumsiness may affect handwriting.
- Use general good early years' practice to develop skills.
- Use lots of visual prompts, e.g. desk prompts to show how letters are formed.
- See Fine and gross motor skills chapter.

Independent writing

Social communication difficulties will impact upon independent writing, i.e. pupils will find difficulty understanding what is expected of them. Their difficulties with social imagination will restrict creative writing, by their inability to perceive something from another person's perspective and to develop imaginative ideas.

There are a number of strategies which can be considered:

- Develop independent sentence writing through pictures/objects, e.g. 'This is a…' as opposed to news writing.
- Cut up sentences that match well-known stories, for pupils to sequence.
- Demonstrate what is required, e.g. the adult writes a sentence and asks the pupil to follow, with a sentence of their own.
- Use digital camera photographs to recall events, e.g. school visits, when writing about the visit.
- Have an individual alphabet chart/word book/dictionary on their table.
- Use storyboards, picture sequences to provide ideas to write about.
- If necessary, suggest choices of sentences, characters, settings or activities for characters.
- Make use of visual prompts to aid writing skills, e.g. a defined area to write in, a red dot where the writing is to start.

Mathematics

Pupils may have significant strengths in the area of mathematics but also some difficulties, which are related to the triad of impairments.

Strengths:

- recognition and ordering of numbers;
- elements requiring rote learning, e.g. multiplication tables;
- basic computational skills which follow a set pattern or sequence;
- recognition of shapes.

Weaknesses:

- using and applying computational skills to solve problems;
- generalising mathematical skills across the curriculum;
- understanding and developing concepts, e.g. bigger, smaller, longer, shorter.

There are a number of strategies which can be considered:

- the use of concrete aids, e.g. coins, counters;
- concepts such as 'more' or 'bigger' can be taught if lots of visual strategies and examples are used;
- the vocabulary used should always be consistent;
- pupils should be taught to generalise their skills, e.g. once they can count bricks, can they count the same number of sweets?
- visual strategies should be considered to aid understanding and recording in all mathematical activities;
- pupils should have opportunities for lots of practice, repetition and the use of practical activities.

Science

Pupils will have strengths and weaknesses in this area:

- language difficulties will inhibit understanding of instructions, health and safety guidelines and concept development;
- topics within the pupil's experience, e.g. the body, will be easier to relate to;
- learning facts will be more possible than developing abstract ideas;
- topics which rely heavily on abstract thought will be more difficult;
- making predictions, testing hypotheses and answering open-ended questions may cause problems.

There are a number of strategies which can be considered:

- use symbols, pictures, written word to demonstrate health and safety guidelines;
- write instructions in order, i.e. as a list;
- use direct questions/cloze procedures/multiple-choice questions;
- use ICT equipment, e.g. video, computer programs, digital cameras.
- use concrete materials to illustrate teaching;
- use templates to support the recording of experiments/activities;
- use adult help to support co-operative working.

RE, PHSE and Citizenship

Difficulties in being able to distinguish between beliefs, facts and opinions may make discussion very difficult and potentially stressful. This will also apply to discussion in other areas of the curriculum. These subjects are useful vehicles for teaching social skills within a small group.

History

Reciting and memorising lists of kings and queens or dates may be relatively simple for the pupil with an ASD. Using empathy as a way through to understanding the human experience of different peoples at different points in time may be more difficult.

There are a number of strategies to support the pupil:

- for younger pupils, use photographs of themselves to sequence timelines;
- use artefacts as concrete examples;
- use videos and TV programmes;
- use timelines in classrooms to demonstrate periods of time;
- use visits with video or digital camera evidence;
- use visiting actors in historical costumes.

Geography

Pupils will find the recognition of countries more easily attainable on a globe. Understanding the concept of distance is more difficult, as is the understanding of other cultures and their way of life.

There are a number of strategies to support the pupil:

- use a globe rather than a map for world issues;
- use videos, TV programmes, photographs;
- build models to demonstrate other cultures.

PE

Difficulties with gross motor co-ordination may lead to fear of heights and being unable to jump over obstacles, the inability to manipulate games equipment. Social problems may lead to difficulties with turn-taking and team games.
(See the chapter on Gross and fine motor skills).

General considerations

In addition, a curriculum for pupils with an ASD should take into consideration the following:

- be pupil centred not subject centred;
- be delivered in a way that is accessible to the pupil;
- promote communication and interaction skills;
- teach life skills and promote independence;
- include a period each day of sustained physical activity;
- reduction of stress by
  - use of ear muffs, plain walls, screens, physical structure;
  - improving coping skills.

Visual strategies

Pupils with an ASD are generally good visual learners and the following strategies will enhance access to understanding and learning.

Visual timetables

Pupils will benefit from the use of a visual timetable to provide structure, in order to reduce anxiety and promote independence.

Visual timetables can be used in the following manner:

- select photographs, pictures, line drawings or symbols with a label, for each activity of the day, e.g. hanging up coat, sitting for Literacy Hour, individual work, playtime, etc. A large and small picture will be required for each activity. Laminate the pictures;

| Music | Playtime | Maths | Dinner |

- encourage the pupil to remove the symbol card and match it to a larger picture which is placed where the activity will take place, e.g. in the story corner;
  - when the activity is completed put the cards in the finished box and accompany with the word 'finished';
  - encourage the pupil to look at what comes next.
- eventually, the pupil can be encouraged to find what comes next independently and go to the task;
- incorporate rewards into the timetable for completion of tasks;
- pupils who have reading skills may move to a timetable or diary, in written form, with the activity crossed out as it is 'finished';
- changes to routines can be introduced by putting a new picture in the timetable. It may help to allow the pupil to take a familiar object to the new activity/event;
- secondary pupils may need a mentor to go through the timetable each morning and to note any changes to the routine.

Visual sequences

Pupils may need a visual timetable to support them through the day, but within that, they may need short intensive visual sequences to help them through specific activities, which they find difficult. This could be times such as assembly, registration, toilet routines, lunchtime, changing for PE, e.g.:

| Shorts | T-shirt | Trainers |

Some parents may find visual structures useful at home, e.g. for the process of preparing for school.

Visual clarity

It is essential that tasks presented to the pupil with an ASD have visual clarity, i.e. it is visually clear what the task involves rather than dependency on verbal instructions.

- Each question/task on a worksheet should be within divisions marked by clear boundaries, e.g.

not this

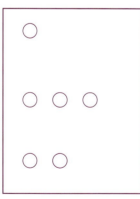

but this

Count and write the number in the box

- Ensure worksheets are uncluttered, i.e. containing the minimum amount of information needed for the pupil to complete the task.
- Make it visually clear where an answer should be placed, i.e. in a precise written or symbol form.
- Demonstrate elements of a task to the pupil within the session.
- Organise a specific place that is consistent for pupils to place finished work, e.g. a tray within the workstation or a box on the teacher's desk.

Fine and gross motor skills

Pupils with an ASD may have delayed development of their fine and gross motor skills, demonstrated in a number of ways:

- have an ungainly gait, when walking or running;
- poor skills in PE;
- be restricted by fine motor skills;
- difficulty with handwriting if they are asked to think of content and presentation together;
- pupils may also tire quickly;
- be anxious, which can also affect the quality of work;
- have difficulty working within a time limit.

There are some strategies which can support limited gross and fine motor skills:

- Encourage a wide range of outdoor play at home and school.
- Encourage participation in PE, particularly those aspects which are more individual, e.g. dance, athletics.
- Team games may cause difficulties linked to the understanding of the rules and the need for co-operation. Rules should be taught.
- Encourage swimming.
- Give opportunities to develop pre-writing skills, e.g. eye/hand co-ordination, activities to develop a pincer grip.
- Use a wide range of multi-sensory activities and materials, e.g. chalks, felt tip pens, a variety of paper, white boards, using fingers in sand to trace writing patterns, (be aware of sensitivity to certain textures).
- Consider the use of the 'Write from the Start' programme to develop writing and perceptual skills.
- Use a structured handwriting scheme.
- Avoid excess copying from the blackboard. Select and highlight a small piece to copy or provide a short version on paper to copy.
- Provide alternative recording methods:
  - use of a word processor;
  - the Widget programme, which uses symbols with words.

Self-esteem

It is important to acknowledge that factors associated with the triad of impairments, may present difficulties with self-esteem that are unique to the autistic spectrum.

- Pupils with an ASD have difficulty recognising that people have their own feelings, thoughts, wishes and intentions.

- Pupils with an ASD have great difficulties in abstracting, feeling and thinking symbolically.

- Many pupils with an ASD are able to interact far more easily with adults than with other pupils.

- Pupils with an ASD are often totally unaware of social rules or may find them illogical.

- Most people with an ASD are able to learn social skills and rules eventually, but only clumsily and with great effort, i.e. social adaptation has to proceed via the intellect.

- Pupils with an ASD often have a need for solitude, a breathing space from social interaction.

- Relationships between pupils with an ASD and their teachers are sometimes impeded by misunderstanding and misinterpretation.

- Some adults misinterpret the behaviour of pupils with ASD and see them as being intentionally rude or naughty.

- Some pupils with an ASD report that they are frequently in trouble, but do not know why. Staff need to understand that a pupil with an ASD is not merely a pupil that needs more discipline, but one that needs an autism-specific approach.

- It may appear that pupils with an ASD have a high level of egocentricity and that they choose to act in this way. This is not the case and they often don't understand their own feelings and behaviour.

- Anxiety and stress within the pupil come from living in a society where everyone is expected to conform to a set pattern.

- Pupils with an ASD are particularly vulnerable to the effects of bullying and are often genuinely traumatised by what others would class as 'mild' teasing.

- Through understanding others we understand ourselves and vice versa, which is difficult for a pupil with an ASD.

A number of strategies can be adopted to support the pupil:

- Avoid making immediate assumptions, but instead, take time to observe and analyse pupil 'behaviour'.
- Extend knowledge of ASD through training, reading factual information, autobiographies.
- Help the pupil learn the social rules.
- Strategies to help to develop self-concept, self-image and self-reference will need to be taught through social skills work and circle time activities.
- Support the pupil if he/she begins to question his/her own difficulties.
- Give the pupil permission to have their breaks in the library or designate an office as a safe place in which to take refuge.
- Develop the understanding of peers through PHSE, circle time.
- Use circle time, 'Social Stories' and social communication groups to help the pupil with an ASD to build relationships.
- Monitor for signs of bullying and isolation of the pupil with an ASD and act accordingly.
- Give support and acceptance to develop a positive self-image.
- Use tightly-structured questions and instructions to allow successful outcomes.
- Teach directly through 'Social Stories' the concept of 'making mistakes'.
- Ensure good home/school relationships.

Home–school liaison

'Parents hold key information and have a critical role to play in their children's education' (Code of Practice 2001)

There are a number of suggestions which may help to foster good home–school partnerships:

- Value the information parents give about their child.
- Share strategies that help to support the child.
- Parents should be aware of the Code of Practice and its implications for them, i.e.
  - have an understanding of the stages within the Code and know which stage their child is at;
  - should be invited to contribute to IEPs, attend review meetings and discuss how they can support the IEP.
- Provide reports for parents before annual reviews.
- Parents should know who to contact if they have concerns about their child, for example:
  - class teacher;
  - special needs co-ordinator;
  - head teacher;
  - special needs governor.
- Parental concerns should be listened to, acknowledged and addressed.
- Parents may be encouraged to become involved in the life of the school, e.g. as reading partners, helpers on school trips, school governors.
- Ensure parents are informed of visits from other professionals, e.g. educational psychologist, speech and language therapist, and receive any relevant reports.
- Consult parents before changes in provision are made.
- Acknowledge possible pressures within the family.
- Use a home/school diary to allow school and home to create a dialogue about the child's home and school life, which will overcome restricted language skills.

The emotional aspects of life with a child with an ASD

Families respond to the diagnosis of ASD in their own individual ways. For all families it is a devastating blow but for some the shock is tempered by the knowledge that at last someone has given a name to their child's problem.

In the months and years that follow, the families start the process of readjustment. Many of the emotions experienced will follow a pattern similar to that of bereavement and each family member may be at a different stage in the process of understanding and accepting the ASD in their child.

- Initial feelings of grief are usually for the child that they thought they would have and now have lost.

- Guilt and anxiety about what went wrong may mean that suggestions of new ways to handle their child are misconstrued as criticism of their parenting.

- Anger may be directed at who or what is felt to be the cause of the child's disability, e.g. MMR, birth trauma.

- Many parents want to search for information about ASD but then feel frustrated at the perceived lack of services.

- Grief may resurface as the parents look to the future and worry about what will become of their child.

- Guilt may also continue to be present, particularly if there are other children in the family. Parents naturally want to do their utmost for their child with an ASD but are also aware of the impact that this is having on family life.

- It is quite natural to want to search for a treatment or cure but it can be a depressing experience when it becomes apparent that there is no cure.

- Acceptance of their child and coming to terms with his/her difficulties follows the realisation that children with an ASD are first and foremost children and, therefore, not so different. They do need more help to overcome their problems.

Siblings of the pupil with an ASD

Children who have a brother or sister with an ASD may need special consideration in school. Their behaviour may be affected, becoming more noisy or withdrawn.

- They may feel that things are not fair and more attention is given to the child with an ASD.

- They may feel resentful that they miss out on things that other families enjoy.

- They may feel embarrassed about their brother's or sister's behaviour.

- They may take undue responsibility for their sibling with an ASD.

- They may worry about their brother or sister.

- They may feel unduly protective towards their brother/sister and extreme anger at children who try to tease or bully.

- Some children may feel guilty about their feelings for their brother/sister.

- They may be teased or bullied because of a sibling with an ASD.

- They may need understanding from staff if their sibling with an ASD causes them to be late, forget PE kit, have homework disturbed.

Individual Educational Plans

When devising IEPs for pupils with an ASD, it is necessary to take into consideration the three aspects of the triad of impairments, as well as individual learning targets. Therefore, there would be at least one target for each area of the triad, i.e.:

- social communication;
- social imagination;
- social interaction.

It is especially important that parents are consulted throughout this process and are encouraged to participate in its implementation. Pupils should also be encouraged to make their contributions to the process.

The following are pen pictures of a varied sample of pupils with an ASD.

Sue

Sue is four years old. She has just started in an early years class. She has no language other than to sing for her own entertainment. She enjoys playing with 'small world people' but in a somewhat rigid manner.

She is unable to be involved in other pupils' play. She does not find it easy to allow adults into play and does not approach adults to make requests or comments.

She finds it difficult to move from her chosen activity to a teacher-directed one.

Some new situations in school have proved difficult, e.g. going into the hall for PE. She does not like loud noise and puts her hands over her ears to block it out.

Ameena

Ameena is nine years old with an ASD. While she doesn't experience any real difficulties academically in the classroom, areas of concern are centred on the triad of impairments.

She is of average ability, is a very good reader, but becomes obsessed with particular topics. She has long-standing hobbies such as an interest in the natural world and will talk endlessly about dinosaurs. She takes things very literally and in a class situation she is eager to do well.

She doesn't have any close friends in her year group but tends to play either in an isolated manner or with younger, less emotionally mature, peers. She often tells the teacher if her peers are not abiding by the class, rules which makes her unpopular.

She frequently makes spontaneous inappropriate comments which are unrelated to the current situation. This disrupts lessons and is distracting to both the teacher and the other pupils.

Tom

Tom is a fourteen-year-old pupil attending a mainstream secondary school. He has delayed literacy and numeracy skills and is generally behind in most of his work.

In the classroom, he can work quite well but at other times he soon becomes wound up and will 'head-bang' on his desk or a nearby wall.

He frequently argues and shouts at peers and will leave the room if challenged.

At lunchtimes there are frequent problems that involve him, particularly in the dinner lines and on the playground.

The following pages give sample Individual Educational Plans to support the pupils described above. A blank IEP sheet is included for use when devising IEPs in school.

School

School action plus

Name: Sue
Date: 16. 9. 02

Date of birth: 5. 4. 98
Review date: 18. 10. 02

Nature of pupil's difficulties: Finds it difficult to allow an adult or child into her play. Finds it difficult to move from her chosen activity to a teacher-directed activity. She does not approach adults to make requests.

Targets	Strategies	Resources	Evaluation
Social interaction To take turns with a child (adult-directed).	Turn-taking activities with an adult, using key words to support, i.e. Sue's turn, Ms K's turn. Sue to take turns with another child, with the adult directing.	Roller balls. Marble runs. Lotto games.	
Social imagination To accept use of the visual timetable to follow the classroom routines.	Use 2 symbols (build up numbers). Adult to give hand over hand prompts to use symbols to direct Sue to the next activity.	Visual timetable.	
Social communication To make spontaneous requests for selected toys.	Introduce PEC with a prompter, build up to 3 symbols. Fade adult prompting. Introduce communication book.	PEC symbols with favourite foods or toys. Communication book. Support from SALT.	

Parental involvement: To use a timetable at home to sequence bedtime routines.
To use PEC book at home to request favourite foods.

School

School action plus

Name: Ameena
Date: 16. 9. 02

Date of birth: 17. 4. 93
Review date: 15. 12. 02

Nature of pupil's difficulties: Tale telling which results in 'falling out' within class. Shouts out inappropriate comments during quiet class times. Talks incessantly about dinosaurs.

Targets	Strategies	Resources	Evaluation
Social interaction To understand that telling tales is not acceptable to her peers.	Support assistant to encourage participation in playground games. Circle time. Use of Social Stories to teach the social rules.	Social Stories Support Staff Games ideas Circle time books	
Social imagination To know when it is OK to talk about dinosaurs.	To make specific times during the day for a small group to share their topics of interest. Opportunities to record their interests.	A visual timetable to show the timing of this session. Member of staff to supervise the group. Tape recorder, computer, pen + paper	
Social communication To put her hand up to address comments to the teacher.	Use of Social Stories to teach the social rules. Rules displayed on the classroom wall, with Ameena's individual prompt card on her desk.	Social Stories Written rules	
Learning targets			

Parental involvement: Parents to talk to Ameena about telling tales if she talks about it at home. To encourage her to talk about dinosaurs only to visitors for a set period.

School

School action plus

Name: Tom
Date: 3. 2. 02

Date of birth: 2. 12. 89
Review date: 15. 4. 04

Nature of pupil's difficulties: Bangs head when challenged by either adults or peers. Argues and shouts, and sometimes leaves the classroom during class discussions. Frequent fights with different peers at lunchtimes.

Targets	Strategies	Resources	Evaluation
Social interaction To participate in more structured lunchtime activities.	Staff to organise structured lunchtime activities.	Encouragement to join clubs, e.g. computer, games, art, reading.	
Social imagination To accept that people may hold a different view.	Use of Social Stories. Circle Time. A designated supervised 'retreat'.	Social Stories. Retreat area.	
Social communication To be able to communicate his frustration verbally.	To give a card/symbol to the teacher which indicates to the teacher that he needs to leave the room and talk to a mentor.	'Time out' card. Member of staff assigned to be a mentor.	
Learning targets			

Parental involvement: Encouragement to join out-of-school clubs (with support).

School

School action plus

Name:
Date:

Date of birth:
Review date:

Nature of pupil's difficulties:

Targets	Strategies	Resources	Evaluation

Parental involvement:

Acknowledgements and useful contacts

Cumine, V., Leach, J. and Stevenson, G. (1998) *Asperger's Syndrome: A Practical Guide for Teachers*, David Fulton Publishers.

Gray, Carol *The New Social Story Book,* Future Horizons.

Hannah, Liz *Teaching Young Children with Autistic Spectrum Disorders to Learn*, National Autistic Society.

Jones, J. (2002) *Educational Provision for Children with Autism and Asperger's Syndrome: Meeting Their Needs*, David Fulton Publishers.

Kingston upon Hull Inclusion Policy Statement (2002).

Jordan, R. and Jones, G. (1999) *Meeting the Needs of Children with Autistic Spectrum Disorders*, David Fulton Publishers.

Leicester City Council and Leicestershire County Council (2001) *Asperger's Syndrome – Practical Strategies for the Classroom: A Teacher's Guide*, The National Autistic Society.

Richman, S. (2001) *Raising a Child with Autism*, Jessica Kingsley Publishers.

Rinaldi, Wendy *Social Use of Language Programme (SULP)*, NFER Nelson.

Sainsbury, C. (2000) *Martian in the Playground*, Lucky Duck Publishing Ltd.

The National Autistic Society (2001) *Approaches to Autism: An Easy to use Guide to Many and Varied Approaches to Autism*, The National Autistic Society.

The National Autistic Society (2000) *The Autism Handbook*, The National Autistic Society.

The National Autistic Society
393 City Road
London EC1V 1NG
020 7833 2299
email nas@nas.org.uk
www.nas.org.uk

Thanks to the pupils of Priory Primary School, Hull for their drawings for the visual timetable.

Some professionals who may be involved with the pupil

Professional	Personnel and contact number
Special Needs Adviser	
Educational Psychologist	
Specialist Outreach Teacher for ASD	
Speech and Language Therapist	
Special Educational Needs Support Service	
Hearing Impairment Service	
School Nurse	
Occupational Therapist	
Social Worker	
Educational Welfare Officer	
Multi-agency link team	
Visual Impairment Service	

What is an Autistic Spectrum Disorder?

The following gives a brief overview of an Autistic Spectrum Disorder.

The term Autistic Spectrum Disorder (ASD) is a broad term used to describe pupils with a range of difficulties such as Asperger's Syndrome, Autism, semantic pragmatic disorder, and pathological demand avoidance syndrome. These difficulties are seen as a continuum and the degree to which pupils are affected will vary significantly. An ASD is biologically based, can affect pupils across the full cognitive range and may be present alongside other disabilities/difficulties.

There are three key areas of impairment associated with ASD: social communication, social interaction and social imagination.

Social communication

Pupils may have difficulty understanding and using:

- the initiation and maintenance of conversations;
- language content and structure;
- volume of speech, intonation and pitch;
- turn-taking in conversations;
- non-verbal communication: facial expression, body language, gesture;
- eye contact.

Some tips to support the pupil:

- keep language clear and simple;
- give time for the pupil to respond;
- teach turn-taking skills;
- use visual prompts;
- avoid sarcasm.

Social interaction

Pupils may have poor social understanding and have difficulties with:

- developing and maintaining relationships (pupils may prefer to be solitary or want to have friendships but lack the skills);
- understanding another person's feelings/perspective;
- working as part of a pair/group/team;
- using appropriate behaviour towards others (peers and adults);
- understanding 'social rules'.

Some tips to support the pupil:

- teach how to play with an adult and then with a peer;
- encourage supported social interaction;
- teach social skills;
- use Social Stories;
- use Circle of friends/buddies;

Social imagination/flexibility of thought

Pupils may

- have difficulty with understanding abstract concepts, e.g. 'more, faith, history';
- have difficulty with work involving creative thinking, e.g. story writing;
- dislike changes in routine;
- have a restricted range of interests;
- display stereotyped body movements, e.g. flapping, rocking;
- find difficulty transferring skills.

Some tips to support the pupil:

- use a visual timetable/diary to show the structure of the day;
- use a calendar to prepare for change;
- give warning of changes – timers/count down;
- use visual cues to develop understanding;
- provide structures/choices to support creative work;
- teach generalisation from one situation to another.

Sensory difficulties

Pupils with an ASD may have sensory difficulties resulting in:

- hyper-sensitivity to sensory information, e.g. noise, light, textures;
- hypo-sensitivity to sensory information, e.g. pain, hunger;
- being mono-channelled;
- easily distracted;
- their sensitivity may fluctuate.

Motivation

Pupils with an ASD may not have the same motivation as others, owing to difficulties with social understanding. Support them by:

- observing the pupil to establish what they are interested in to use as an appropriate reward;
- including the reward in the visual timetable to reward a completed task;
- rewarding frequently.

Strengths

Pupils with an ASD will have a variety of strengths, varying from person to person, which will help to access the curriculum, including:

- ability to process visual information;
- good use of ICT;
- ability to focus on detail;
- ability to concentrate on an activity of interest;
- good at learning rote information.

ASD is a lifelong disability but there are many strategies that parents, professionals and the pupils themselves can use to manage the difficulties presented.

Improve your support for pupils with SEN with other books in this series...

The books in this series gather together all the vital knowledge and practical support that schools need to meet specific special needs. Information is simply explained and clearly sign-posted so that practitioners can quickly access what they need to know. Each book describes a specific area of special educational need and explains how it might present difficulties for pupils within the school setting. Checklists and photocopiable forms are provided to help save time and develop good practice.

Supporting Children with Behaviour Difficulties
£12.00 • Paperback • 64 A4 pages • 1-84312-228-6 • 2004

Supporting Children with Motor Co-ordination Difficulties
£12.00 • Paperback • 64 A4 pages • 1-84312-227-8 • 2004

Supporting Children with Fragile X Syndrome
£10.00 • Paperback • 64 A4 pages • 1-84312-226-X • 2004

Supporting Children with Speech and Language Difficulties
£10.00 • Paperback • 144 A4 pages • 1-84312-225-1 • 2004

Supporting Children with Medical Conditions
£20.00 • Paperback • 144 A4 pages • 1-84312-224-3 • 2004

Supporting Children with Epilepsy
£10.00 • Paperback • 64 A4 pages • 1-84312-223-5 • 2004

Supporting Children with Dyslexia
£10.00 • Paperback • 48 A4 pages • 1-84312-222-7 • 2004

Supporting Children with Down's Syndrome
£10.00 • Paperback • 48 A4 pages • 1-84312-221-9 • 2004

Supporting Children with Cerebral Palsy
£10.00 • Paperback • 48 A4 pages • 1-84312-220-0 • 2004

Supporting Children with Autistic Spectrum Disorder
£10.00 • Paperback • 64 A4 pages • 1-84312-219-7 • 2004

Supporting Children with Asthma
£10.00 • Paperback • 48 A4 pages • 1-84312-218-9 • 2004

1-84312-373-8 Supporting Children with ... (11 Volume set) £99.00

ORDER FORM

Qty	ISBN	Title	Price	Subtotal
	1-84312-218-9	Supporting Children with Asthma	£10.00	
	1-84312-219-7	Supporting Children with ASD	£10.00	
	1-84312-228-6	Supporting Children with Behaviour Ds	£12.00	
	1-84312-220-0	Supporting Children with Cerebral Palsy	£10.00	
	1-84312-221-9	Supporting Children with Down's Syndrome	£10.00	
	1-84312-222-7	Supporting Children with Dyslexia	£10.00	
	1-84312-223-5	Supporting Children with Epilepsy	£10.00	
	1-84312-226-X	Supporting Children with Fragile X Syndrome	£10.00	
	1-84312-224-3	Supporting Children with Medical Conditions	£20.00	
	1-84312-227-8	Supporting Children with MCDs	£12.00	
	1-84312-225-1	Supporting Children with S&L Difficulties	£10.00	
	1-84312-373-8	Supporting Children with ... (11 Volume set)	£99.00	
	1-84312-355-X	SEN Catalogue	FREE	
		Postage and Packing: FREE to schools, LEAs and other institutions. £2.50 per order for private/personal orders. Prices and publication dates are subject to change.	P&P	
			TOTAL	

Postage and Packing: FREE to schools, LEAs and other institutions.
£2.50 per order for private/personal orders.
Prices and publication dates are subject to change.

Please complete delivery details:

Name: ....

Organisation: ....

Address: ....

....

....

....

Postcode: ....

Tel: ....

Email: ....

☐ Please add me to your email mailing list

Payment:
☐ Please invoice *(applicable to schools, LEAs and other institutions)*
☐ I enclose a cheque payable to David Fulton Publishers Ltd *(include postage and packing if applicable)*
☐ Please charge to my credit card *(Visa/Barclaycard, Access/Mastercard, American Express, Switch, Delta)*

card number ☐☐☐☐☐☐☐☐☐☐☐☐☐☐☐☐☐☐☐

expiry date ☐☐☐☐

(Switch customers only) valid from ☐☐☐☐   Issue number ☐☐

Send your order to our distributors:

HarperCollins Publishers
Customer Service Centre
Westerhill Road • Bishopbriggs
Glasgow • G64 2QT

Tel. 0870 787 1721

Fax. 0870 787 1723

or order online at
www.fultonpublishers.co.uk